DIY Crafts

2nd Edition

Make Your Own Lip Balm with These 35 Quick & Easy Recipes!

by Kitty Moore

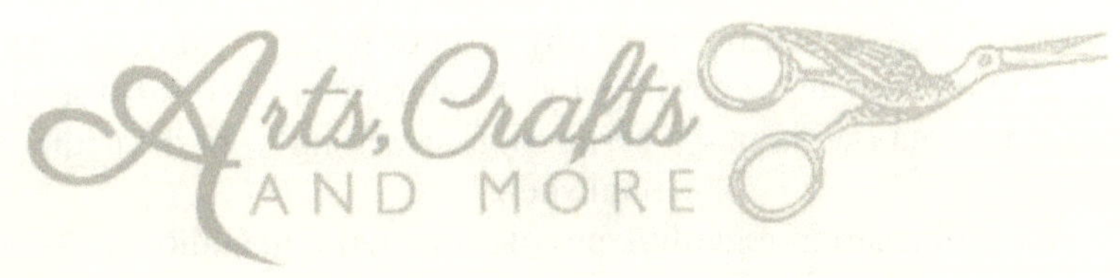

Table of Contents

Introduction

We all need a touch of natural, sweet smelling and moisturizing oils on our lips to keep them safe from the harshness of the elements.

This is where this book comes in. It contains diverse lip balm recipes that you can play around with to your heart's desire as you get ready to protect and nourish your lips.

You can say goodbye to dry, cracking, flaking or bleeding lips because all the lip balm recipes in this book contain ingredients that are meant to ensure you have the best feeling and looking lips ever.

The book carries bonuses with it, the recipes are not only good for your lips, but for your pocket and your time as well.

There is one thing to note, if your lip balm is too thick for you, add a little vegetable oil, if too thick, add the thickening ingredient which is either beeswax or candelille wax.

1. Coco-mint Lip Balm

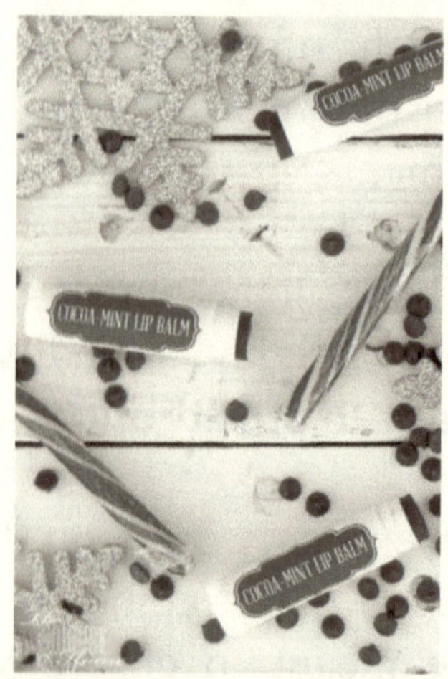

Materials

- 2 tablespoon each of coconut oil and grated beeswax

- 1 tablespoon olive oil

- 2 teaspoon cocoa butter

- 1 teaspoon vitamin E

- 10 drops peppermint oil

Directions

1. Get container ready for balm. Melt coconut oil, cocoa butter, olive oil and beeswax in a saucepan over low heat.

2. Add vitamin E and peppermint oil into the pot, stirring continuously until thoroughly mixed.

3. Remove from heat and **quickly** pour into pre-made containers to solidify.

2. Almond Rose Lip Balm

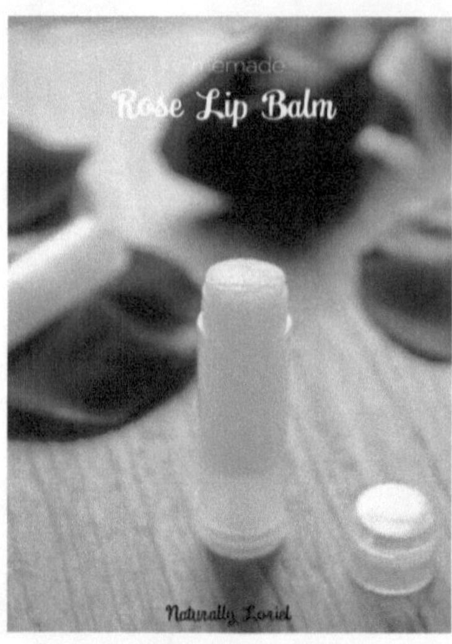

Materials

- 1 tablespoon each of coconut oil and grated beeswax

- 2 tablespoons almond oil

- ½ teaspoon vitamin E

- 5 drops rose oil

- A tiny piece of your favorite lipstick

Directions

1. Prepare the lip balm containers. Place coconut oil, beeswax and piece of lipstick into a small, thick based saucepan.

2. Melt over very low heat stirring continuously.

3. Stir in the almond oil, vitamin E and drops of rose oil and mix thoroughly.

4. When ingredients are fully incorporated, remove from heat.

5. Pour into prepared containers and allow to cool down.

3. Coconut & Tea Tree Oil Lip Balm

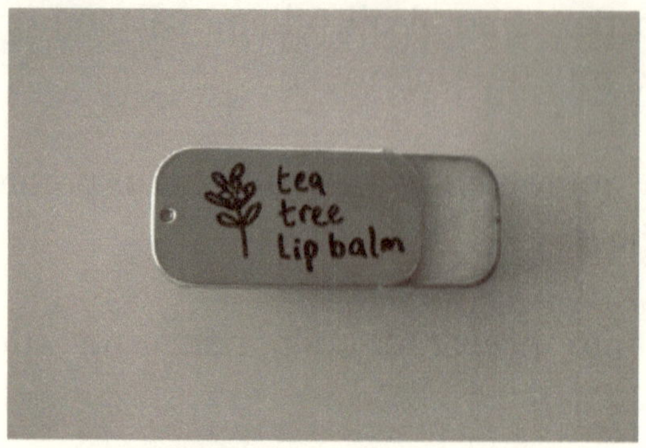

Materials

- 3 tablespoons grated beeswax

- 2 tablespoons coconut oil

- 1 teaspoon vitamin E oil

- 3 drops tea tree oil

Directions

1. Make the containers ready. Melt the beeswax and coconut oil in a double boiler or over boiling water.

2. Stir in vitamin E and tea tree oil and mix together thoroughly.

3. Pour mixture into your pre-made containers.

4. Almond Honey Lip Balm

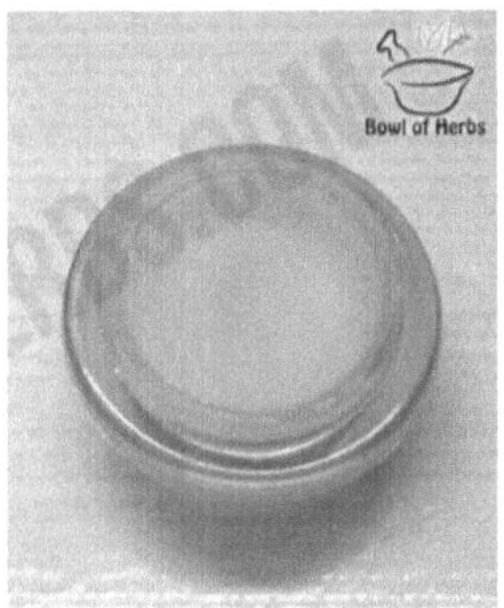

Materials

- 4 tablespoon almond oil

- 1 tablespoon beeswax oil

- 1 teaspoon each of honey and cocoa powder

- ½ teaspoon vitamin E

- 8 drops vanilla oil

- 1 teaspoon hibiscus powder (optional, for tint)

Directions

1. Prepare your containers.

2. Melt the oils, honey and beeswax on extra low heat.

3. Stir until completely mixed and beeswax is melted.

4. Remove from heat and quickly whisk in Vitamin, cocoa powder and hibiscus powder (if you are using).

5. When thoroughly mixed, pour into your pre-made containers.

5. Coconut Lavender Lip Balm

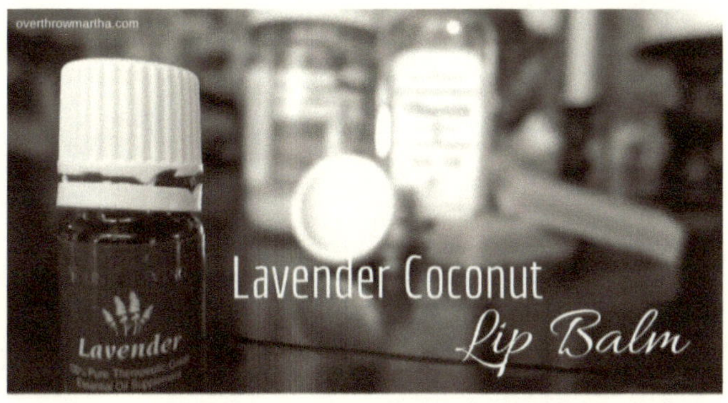

Materials

- 2 tablespoon each of beeswax and coconut oil

- 1 tablespoon avocado oil

- 2 teaspoon cocoa butter

- 1 teaspoon vitamin E

- 10 drops lavender oil

Directions

1. Get container ready for balm. Melt coconut oil, cocoa butter, avocado oil and beeswax in a saucepan over low heat.

2. Add vitamin E and lavender oil into the pot, and stir continuously until completely mixed.

3. Remove from heat and **quickly** pour into pre-made containers to solidify.

I have included a bonus just for you…

FOR A LIMITED TIME ONLY – Get my best-selling book "DIY Crafts: The 100 Most Popular Crafts & Projects That Make Your Life Easier" absolutely FREE!

Readers who have downloaded the bonus book as well have seen the greatest changes in their crafting abilities and have expanded their repertoire of crafts – so it is *highly recommended* to get this bonus book today!

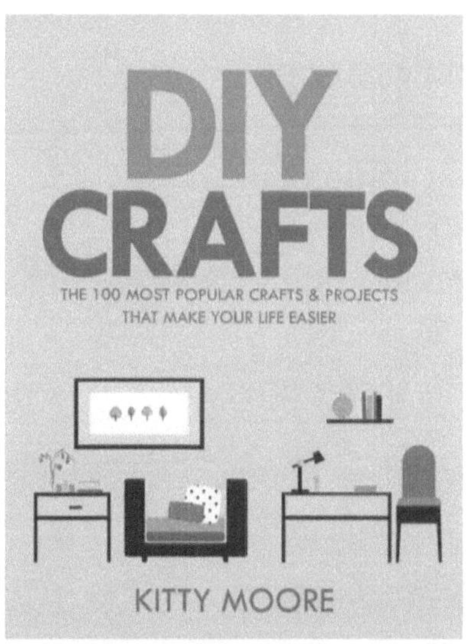

Get your free copy at:

ArtsCraftsAndMore.com/Bonus

6. Jojoba & Carrot Seed Lip Balm

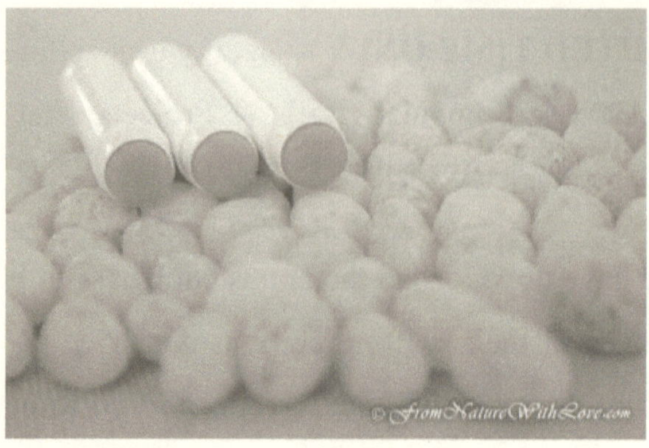

Materials

- 2 tablespoon castor oil

- 1 tablespoon jojoba oil

- 1 ¼ tablespoon grated beeswax

- 1 tablespoon shea butter

- 5 drops vitamin E

- 5 drops carrot seed oil

Directions

1. Prepare the containers. Heat together the castor oil, jojoba oil, beeswax and shea butter in a double boiler until it all melts.

2. Separate the boilers and stir in vitamin E and carrot seed oils.

3. When thoroughly mixed, pour into prepared containers and leave to cool.

7. Lanolin & Grape Seed Lip Balm

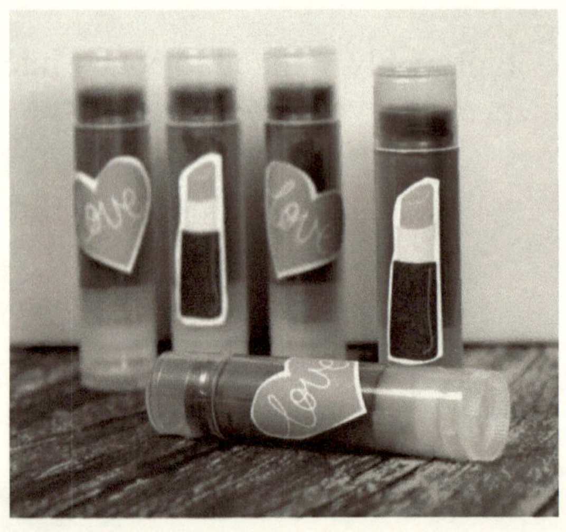

Materials

- 2 tablespoon lanolin

- 2 tablespoon cocoa butter

- 2 tablespoon beeswax

- 2 tablespoon linseed oil

- 2 tablespoons grape seed oil

- 5 drops peppermint oil

- 10 drops vitamin E oil

- Alkanet root powder

Directions

1. Prepare your lip balm containers. Use a double boiler to melt the ingredients except grape seed oil and the drops of peppermint and vitamin E oils.

2. When thoroughly melted, add alkanet root powder and mix thoroughly.

3. Remove from heat and wipe bottom of top boiler to prevent water getting into balm when pouring.

4. Add peppermint oil, vitamin E oil and grape seed oil and continue mixing briskly.

5. Pour into ready prepared containers and leave to cool.

8. Glossy Rose Jojoba Lip Balm

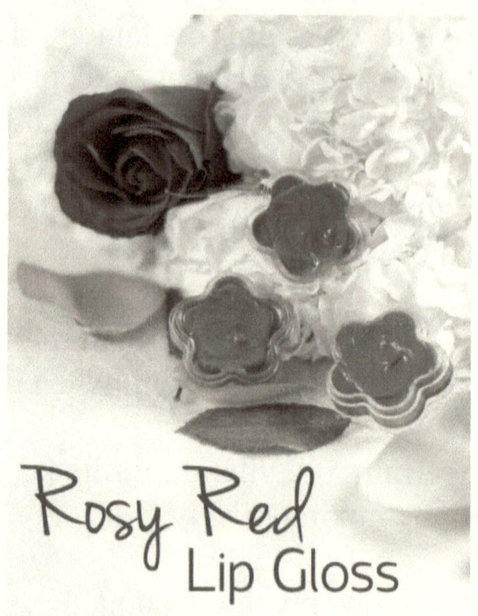

Materials

- 1 tablespoon avocado oil

- 2 tablespoon jojoba oil

- ¾ tablespoon candelilla wax

- 1 tablespoon shea butter

- 5 drops vitamin E

- 3 drops rose oil

Directions

1. Prepare the containers. Heat together the avocado oil, jojoba oil, candelilla wax and shea butter in a double boiler until it all ingredients melt.

2. Separate the boilers and stir in vitamin E and rose oils.

3. When thoroughly mixed, pour into prepared containers and leave to cool preferable overnight.

9. Linseed & Honey Lip Balm

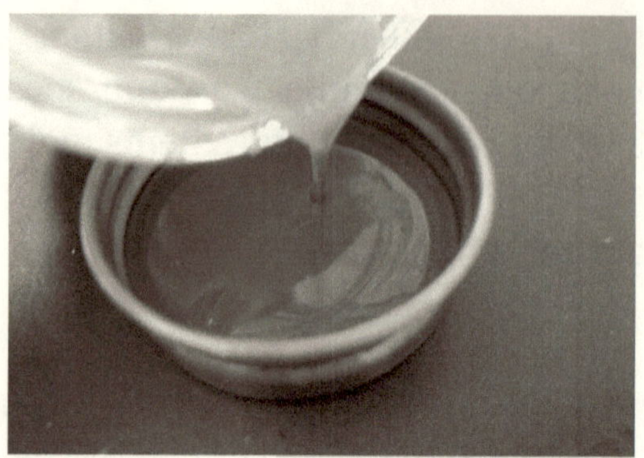

Materials

- 1 tablespoon lanolin

- 1 tablespoon coconut oil

- 1 tablespoon Linseed oil

- 1 ½ teaspoon honey

- 1/2 tablespoon candelilla wax

- 3 drops rose oil

- 10 drops vitamin E

- A small piece of your favorite lipstick

Directions

1. Ensure your lip balm containers are ready. Put all your ingredients except honey and rose oil in a thick base saucepan.

2. Melt on low heat until mixture completely liquefies. Remove from heat and mix thoroughly. Add honey and drops of rose oil and mix briskly.

3. When thoroughly mixed, pour into ready-made containers. Allow to set preferably overnight.

10. Lanolin & Sweet Orange Lip Balm

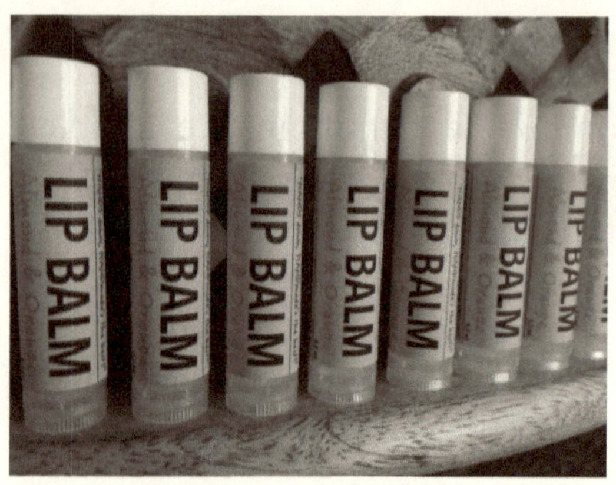

Materials

- 2 tablespoon lanolin oil

- 2 tablespoon sunflower oil

- 3 teaspoons of honey

- 2 tablespoon beeswax

- 10 drops sweet orange oil

Directions

1. Ready your lip balm containers. Place all your ingredients save for honey and orange oil in a microwave safe bowl.

2. Microwave on low heat until mixture becomes liquid. Remove from microwave and thoroughly mix.

3. Add honey and drops of orange oil and mix briskly and make sure it is thoroughly mixed.

4. Pour into prepared containers and wait for balm to cool down.

11. Castor Oil & Peppermint Lip Balm

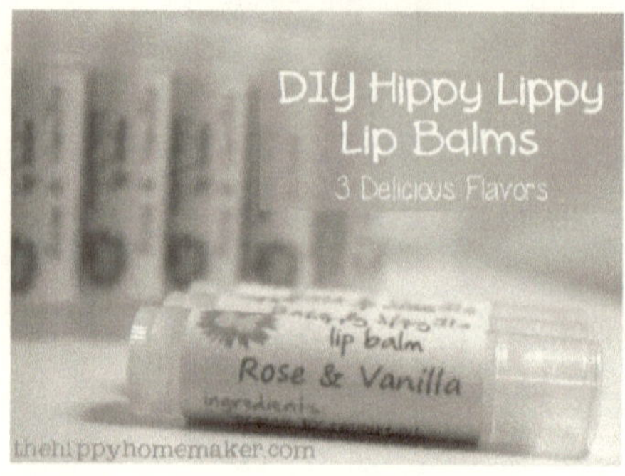

Materials

- 2 tablespoon shea butter

- 2 tablespoon cocoa butter

- 2 tablespoon beeswax

- 4 tablespoon castor oil

- 5 drops peppermint

- Alkanet root powder

Directions

1. Prepare your lip balm containers. Use a double boiler to melt the first three ingredients.

2. When thoroughly melted, add alkanet root powder and mix.

3. Add peppermint oil and Caster oil and continue
   mixing briskly. Pour into prepared containers and
   allow to set.

12. Castor Oil & Chamomile Lip Balm

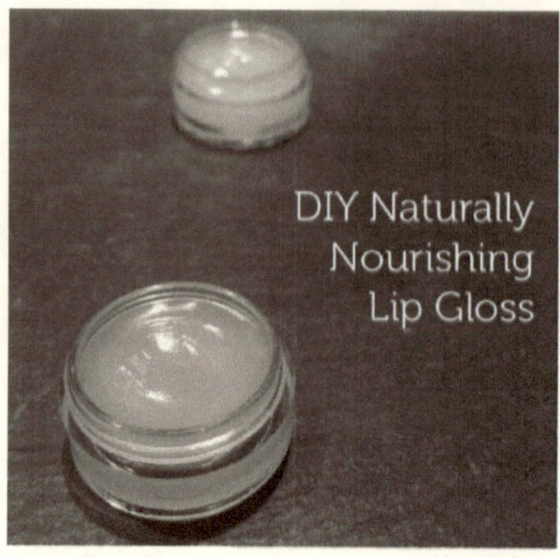

Materials

- 1 tablespoon olive oil

- 2 tablespoon castor oil

- ½ tablespoon candelilla wax

- 1 tablespoon shea butter

- 5 drops vitamin E

- 5 drops chamomile oil

Directions

1. Get the lip balm containers ready. Heat together the castor oil, olive oil, candelilla wax and shea butter in a microwave, on medium heat for 45 seconds.

2. Take container you are using and stir in vitamin E
   and carrot seed oils.

3. When thoroughly mixed, pour into prepared
   containers and leave to set preferably overnight.

13. Lanolin & Castor Oil Lip Balm

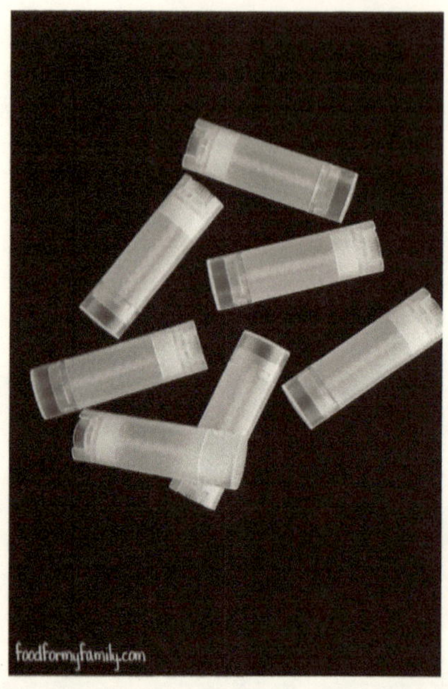

Materials

- 2 tablespoon castor oil

- 1 tablespoon coconut oil

- 1 ¼ tablespoon grated beeswax

- 1 tablespoon lanolin

- 5 drops vitamin E

- 3 drops peppermint oil

Directions

1. Get the containers ready. Heat together the castor oil, coconut oil, beeswax and lanolin in a thick-based pan over very low heat until everything melts.

2. Remove from heat and stir in vitamin E and peppermint oils.

3. When thoroughly mixed, pour into prepared containers and leave to cool.

14. Honey Peppermint Lip Balm

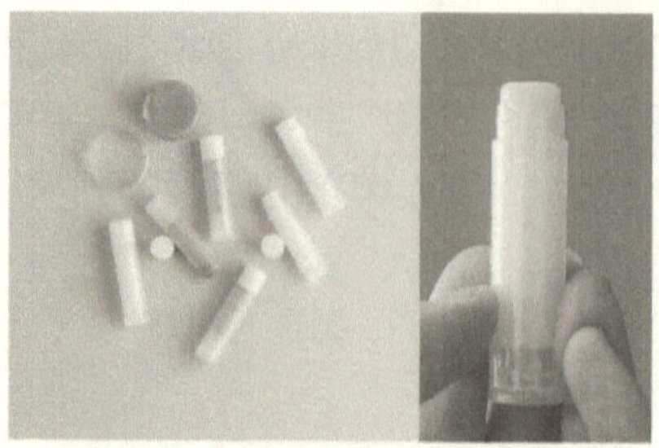

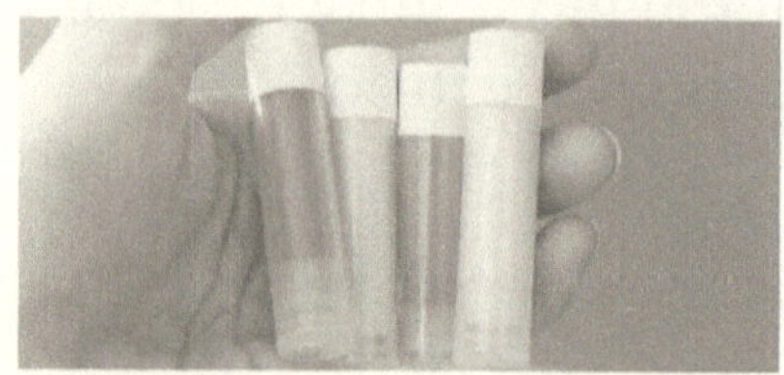

Materials

- 2 teaspoons petroleum jelly

- 5 drops of peppermint oil

- 1 teaspoon honey

- 5 drops vitamin E

- Hibiscus powder

Directions

1. Prepare the lip balm containers. Melt the petroleum jelly in a double boiler.

2. Put the drops of vitamin E and those of peppermint oil and mix thoroughly.

3. Add the honey and continue mixing so that honey does not set.

4. Add the hibiscus powder and mix thoroughly.

5. Pour the mixture into prepared containers and allow it to set.

15. Jojoba & Lavender Oil Lip Balm

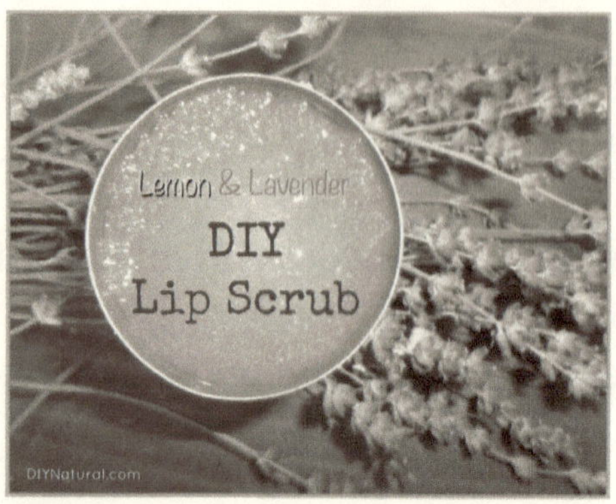

Materials

- 2 tablespoon jojoba oil

- 1 tablespoon candelilla wax

- 1 tablespoon olive oil

- 2 teaspoon cocoa butter

- 1/2 teaspoon vitamin E

- 5 drops lavender oil

Directions

1. Ready the container for balm. Heat jojoba oil, cocoa butter, olive oil and candelilla wax in a saucepan over low heat.

2. Add vitamin E oil and lavender oil drops into the pot, stirring continuously until well mixed.

3. Remove from heat and pour into prepared containers to cool and set.

16. Olive Honey Lip Balm

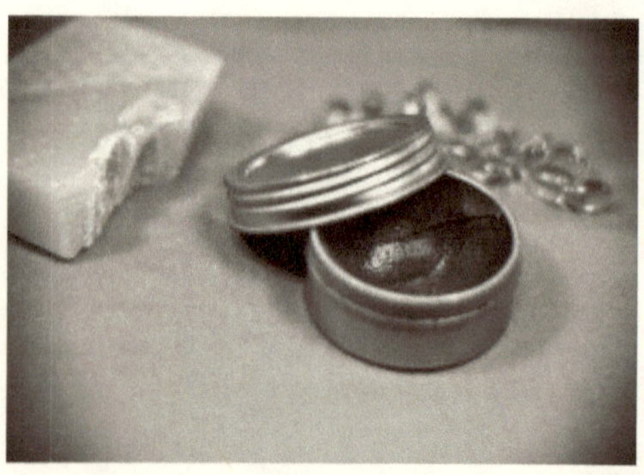

Materials

- 1 tablespoon shea butter oil

- 1 tablespoon olive oil

- 1 ½ teaspoon honey

- 1 tablespoon beeswax

- 10 drops rose oil

Directions

1. Get your lip balm containers ready. Put all your ingredients except honey and rose oil in a microwave safe bowl.

2. Microwave on low heat until mixture completely melts.

3. Take out from microwave and mix thoroughly.

4. Add honey and drops of rose oil and mix briskly
   until thoroughly mixed.

5. Pour into ready-made containers.

17. Cocomile Lip Balm

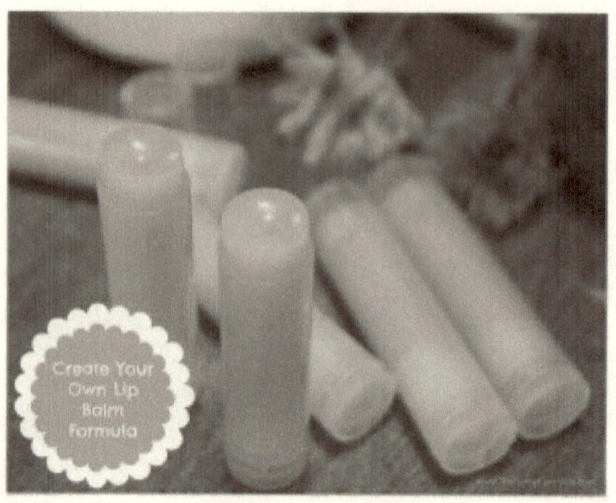

Materials

- 1 tablespoon olive oil

- 1 tablespoon coconut oil

- 1 tablespoon grated beeswax

- 10 drops vitamin E

- 5 drops chamomile oil

Directions

1. Make your lip balm containers ready. Melt beeswax and coconut oil in a small saucepan over extremely low heat.

2. Stir in the olive oil, and put the drops of chamomile
    oil and vitamin E and mix well.

3. Remove from heat. Pour into ready-made containers
    and allow to cool and to set.

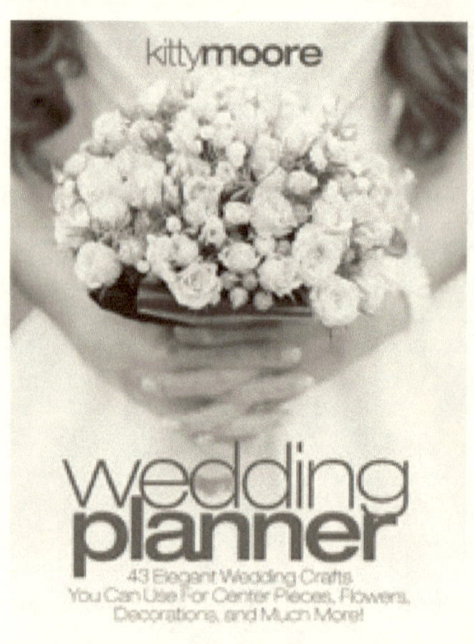

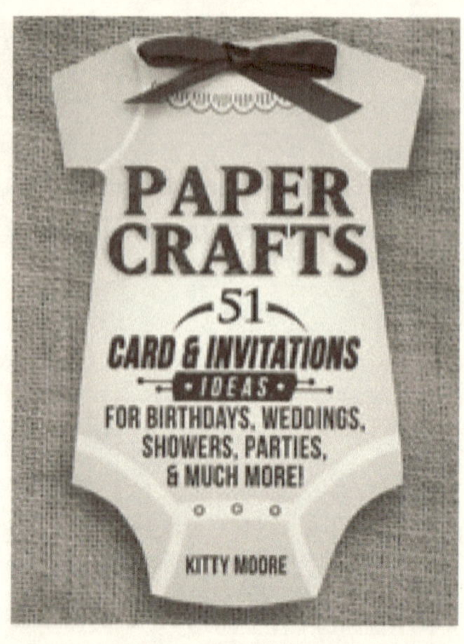

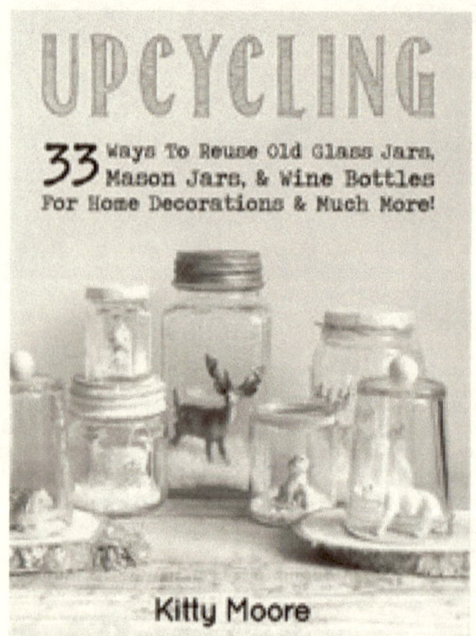

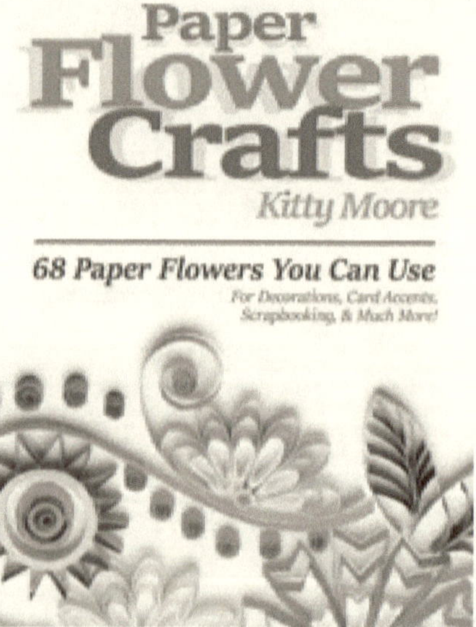

Check out Kitty's books at:

ArtsCraftsAndMore.com/go/books

18. Coconut & Citrus Lip Balm

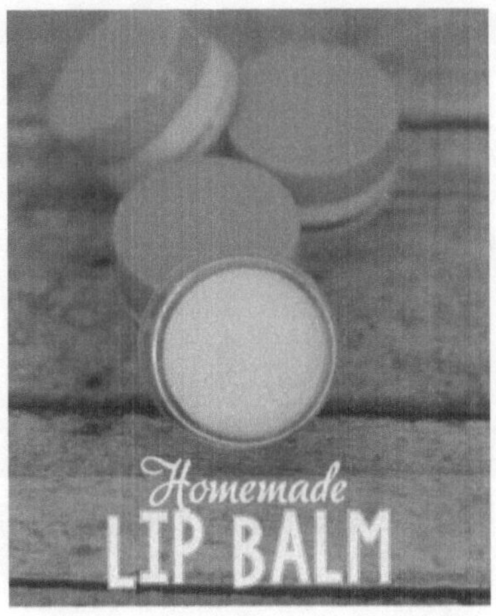

Materials

- 3 tablespoon avocado oil

- 2 tablespoon coconut oil

- 1½ tablespoon beeswax

- 1 tablespoon cocoa butter

- 10 drops of citrus oil

- ½ teaspoon of vitamin E

Directions

1. Ready the containers for balm. Melt the coconut oil in a double base saucepan over low heat.

2. Add the avocado oil and mix thoroughly.

3. Add the bees wax and cocoa, stirring well until mixture is fully melted.

4. Remove from heat and add rose oil and vitamin E stirring well.

5. Pour into prepared containers.

19. Lanolin & Sweet Grape Lip Balm

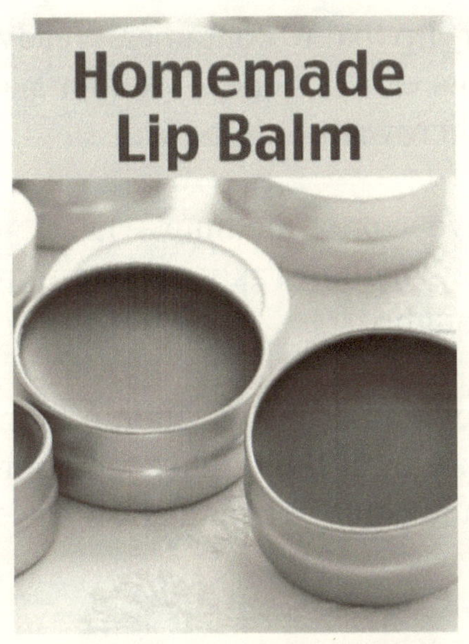

Materials

- 1 tablespoon lanolin

- 1 tablespoon linseed oil

- 1 teaspoon grape seed oil

- 1 ½ teaspoon honey

- ½ tablespoon beeswax

- ½ teaspoon vitamin E

- 5 drops peppermint oil

43

Directions

1. Get your lip balm containers ready. Put all your ingredients except honey, vitamin E and peppermint oil in a microwave safe bowl.

2. Microwave on medium heat until mixture completely melts. Take out from microwave and mix thoroughly.

3. Add honey and drops of vitamin E and rose oils and mix briskly until thoroughly incorporated. Pour into ready-made containers and allow to set.

20. Honey Chamomile Lip Balm

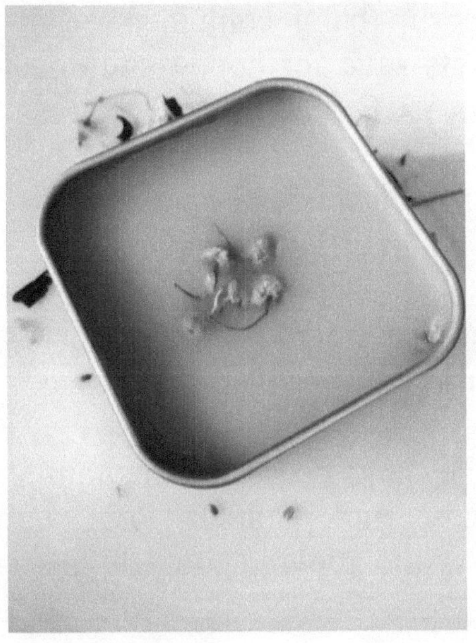

Materials

- 1 tablespoon sunflower oil

- 1 tablespoon jojoba oil

- 1 ½ teaspoon honey

- 1 tablespoon beeswax

- 4 drops chamomile oil

- Alkanet root powder (optional, for tint)

Directions

1. Get your lip balm containers ready. Put all your ingredients save for honey and chamomile oil in a microwave safe bowl.

2. Microwave on medium heat for 30 seconds or until mixture completely melts.

3. Take out from microwave and thoroughly mix in the alkanet root powder if you are using.

4. Add honey and drops of chamomile oil and mixd until fully incorporated. Pour into ready-made containers and allow to cool and harden.

21. Almond & Carrot Seed Lip Balm

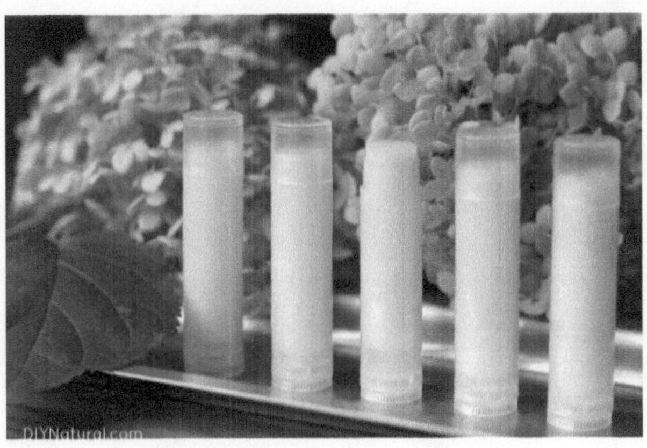

Materials

- 4 tablespoons almond oil

- 1 tablespoon beeswax

- 1 teaspoon each of honey and cocoa powder

- ½ teaspoon vitamin E

- 8 drops carrot seed oil

- 1 teaspoon alkanet root powder (optional, for tint)

Directions

1. Make your containers ready.

2. Melt the oils, honey and beeswax in a double boiler.

3. Stir until completely mixed and beeswax is melted.

4. Whisk in Vitamin, cocoa powder and coconut root powder (if you are using).

5. Pour into your pre-made containers once thoroughly mixed.

22. Lanolin & Tea Tree Lip Balm

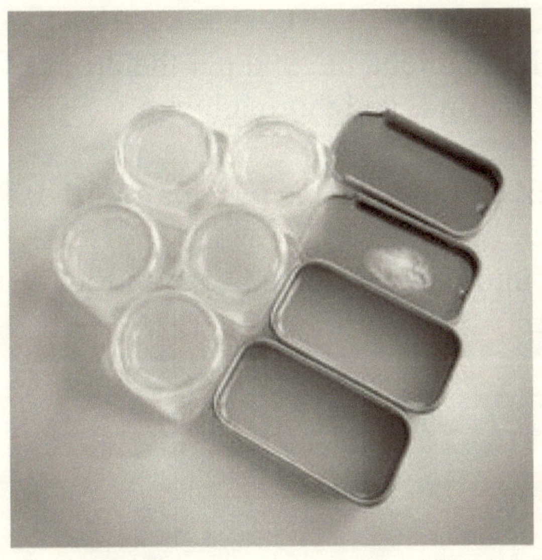

Materials

- 1 tablespoon jojoba oil

- 1 tablespoon lanolin

- 1/2 tablespoon candelilla wax

- 5-8 drops vitamin E

- 5 drops tea tree oil

Directions

1. Prepare your lip balm containers.

2. Melt candelilla wax and lanolin in a small saucepan
    over extremely low heat.

3. Stir in the jojoba oil, and put the drops of tea tree oil
    and vitamin E and thoroughly mix.

4. Remove from heat and mix for a further 10 seconds.

5. Pour into prepared containers and leave to cool and
    to set.

23. Delicious Rose Lip Balm

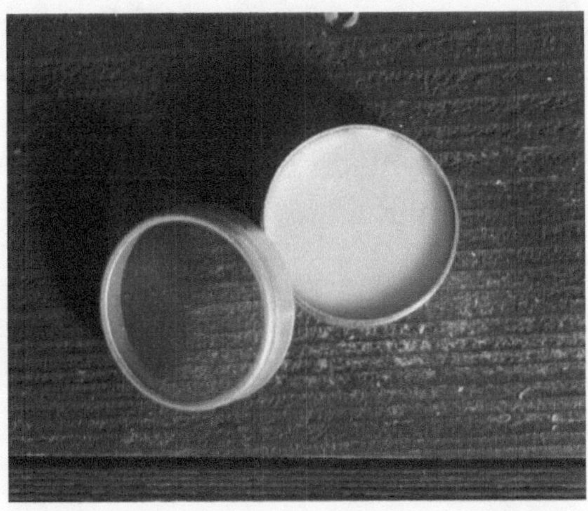

Materials

- 1 tablespoon sunflower oil

- 1 tablespoon shea butter

- 1 tablespoon grated beeswax

- 10 drops vitamin E

- 5 drops rose oil

Directions

1. Make your lip balm containers ready.

2. Melt beeswax and shea butter in a double boiler.

3. Stir in the sunflower oil, and put the drops of rose oil and vitamin E.

4. Mix thoroughly and remove from heat.

5. Pour into ready-made containers and allow to cool and to set overnight.

24. Avocado & Honey Lip Balm

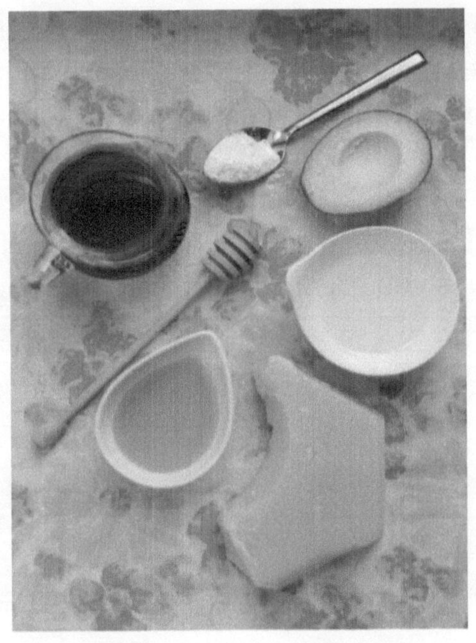

Materials

- 1 tablespoon avocado oil

- 1 tablespoon jojoba oil

- 1 ½ teaspoon honey

- ½ tablespoon candelilla wax

- 3 drops carrot seed oil

- Hibiscus powder (optional, for tint)

Directions

1. Get your lip balm containers ready. Put avocado oil, jojoba oil, candelilla wax except in a microwave safe bowl.

2. Microwave on low heat until mixture completely melts. Take out from microwave and stir in hibiscus powder if you are using, stirring thoroughly.

3. Add honey and drops of carrot seed oil and mix briskly until thoroughly mixed. Pour into prepared containers.

25. Almolin Lip Balm

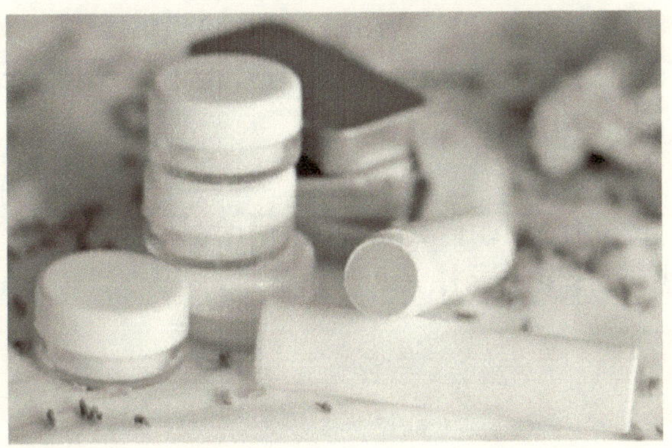

Materials

- 3 tablespoon almond oil

- 2 tablespoon lanolin

- 1½ tablespoon beeswax

- 1 tablespoon cocoa butter

- 1-12 drops of tea tree oil

- 1 teaspoon of vitamin E

- Hibiscus powder (optional, for tint)

Directions

1. Make the containers ready. Melt the lanolin in a double boiler.

2. Mix in the almond oil, stirring.

3. Stir in the bees' wax, cocoa butter and hibiscus powder if you are using, until mixture is fully melted and mixed.

4. Add tea tree oil and vitamin E stir well. Pour into containers and allow to cool.

26. Avo & Vanilla Lip Balm

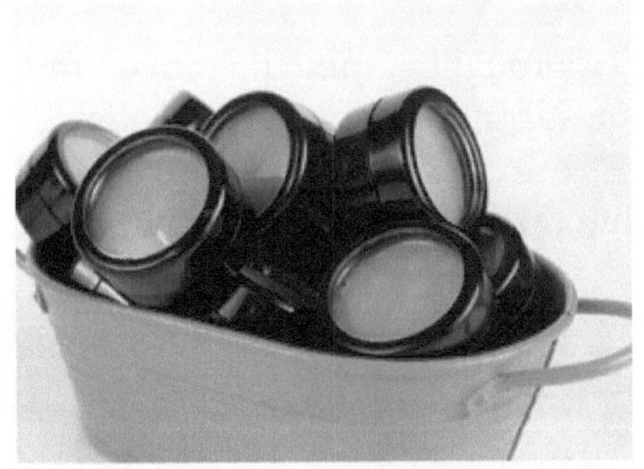

Materials

- 2 tablespoon avocado oil

- 2 tablespoon lanolin

- 2 tablespoon grated beeswax

- 8 drops vitamin E

- 5 drops vanilla oil

Directions

1. Make your lip balm containers ready.

2. Melt beeswax and avocado oil in a small saucepan over very low heat.

3. Add the avocado oil, and put the drops of vanilla oil and vitamin E, stirring.

4. When thoroughly mixed, move from heat and continue stirring for about 3 seconds.

5. Pour into ready-made containers and allow to cool.

27. Coconut & Green Tea Lip Balm

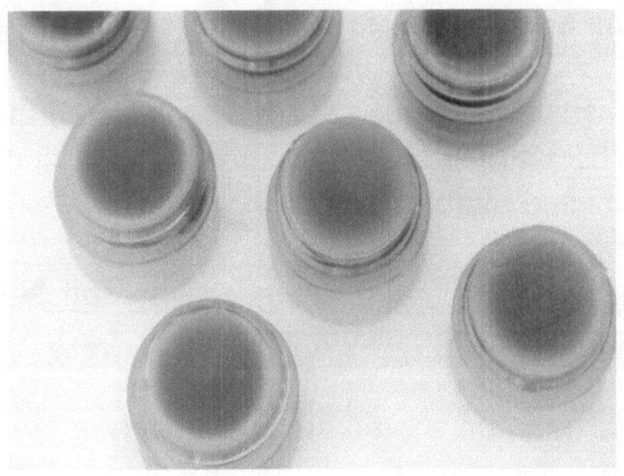

Materials

- 2½ tablespoon coconut oil

- 1 tablespoon each of grated cocoa butter and dried green tea

- ½ teaspoon vitamin E oil

- 3 drops lavender oil

- Alkanet root powder (optional for tint)

Directions

1. Prepare your containers. Melt the coconut oil in a double boiler.

2. When it liquefies, add dried green tea and stir well. Leave it in the boiler for 45 minutes then strain using a fine mesh sieve.

3. Make sure no dried tea residue is left in the pot and put back the mixture. Add cocoa butter and stir till it melts and remove from heat.

4. Add vitamin E and lavender oils and stir briskly. Pour into prepared containers.

Note: This lip balm should always be kept in a cool place lest it runs because the key ingredient, coconut oil, liquefies pretty fast.

28. Coconut & Vanilla Lip Balm

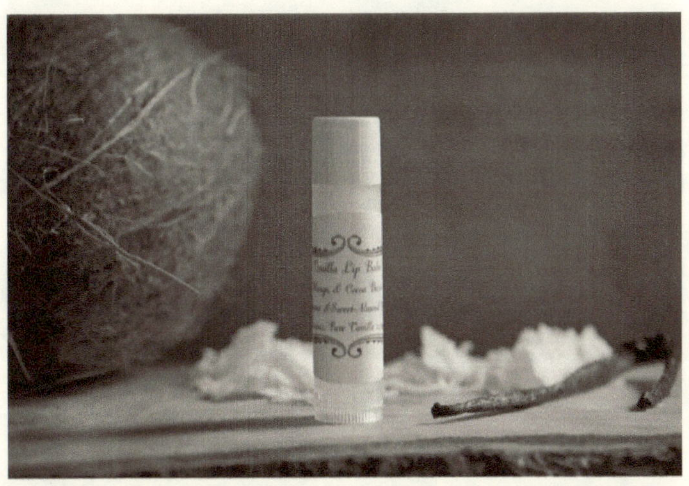

Materials

- 2 tablespoon each of coconut oil and grated beeswax

- 1 tablespoon jojoba oil

- 2 teaspoon shea butter

- 5 -10 drops vitamin E

- 5 drops vanilla oil

Directions

1. Get container ready for balm. Melt coconut oil, shea butter, jojoba oil and beeswax in a thick based saucepan over very low heat.

2. Mix in the drops of vitamin E oil and peppermint oil into the pot, stirring continuously until fully incorporated.

3. Remove from heat and pour into ready-made containers to cool.

29. Coconut & Almond Oil Lip Balm

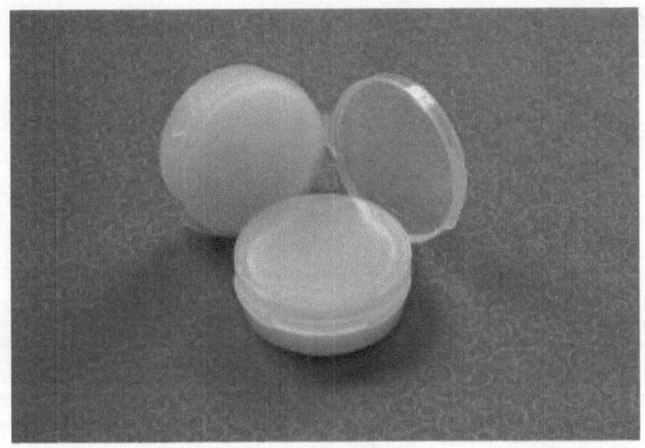

Materials

- 3 tablespoon almond oil

- 2 tablespoon coconut oil

- 1½ tablespoon beeswax

- 1 tablespoon cocoa butter

- 10 drops of rose oil

- ½ teaspoon of vitamin E

Directions

1. Prepare the containers. Melt the coconut oil in a double base saucepan over low heat.

2. Add the almond oil and mix briskly. Stir in the bees wax and cocoa until mixture is fully melted and mixed.

3. Remove from heat and add rose oil and vitamin E stir well. Pour into ready-made containers.

30. Jojoba & Tea Tree Lip Balm

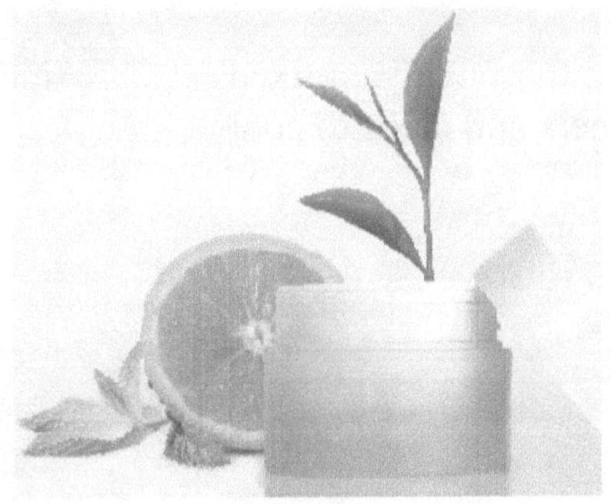

Materials

- 2 tablespoon almond oil

- 1 tablespoon jojoba oil

- 2/3 tablespoon grated candelilla wax

- 1 tablespoon coconut oil

- 5 drops vitamin E

- 5 drops tea tree oil

Directions

1. Prepare the containers. Heat together the almond oil, jojoba oil, candelilla wax and coconut oil in a double boiler until it all melts.

2. Separate the boilers and stir in vitamin E and tea tree oils.

3. When thoroughly mixed, pour into prepared containers and leave to cool.

31. Quick Almond & Coconut Lip Balm

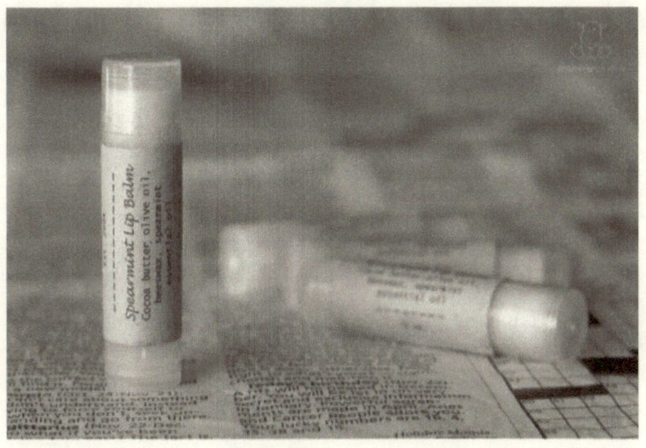

Materials

- 1 tablespoon coconut oil

- 1 tablespoon almond oil

- 1 ½ teaspoon honey

- 1 tablespoon beeswax

- 5 – 8 drops sweet orange oil

Directions

1. Get your lip balm containers ready. Put all your ingredients except honey and orange oil in a microwave safe bowl.

2. Microwave on low heat until mixture liquefies.

3. Take out of microwave and mix thoroughly.

4. Add honey and drops of orange oil and mix briskly until thoroughly mixed.

5. Pour into ready-made containers and wait for balm to cool down.

32. Coconut & Olive Oil Lip Balm

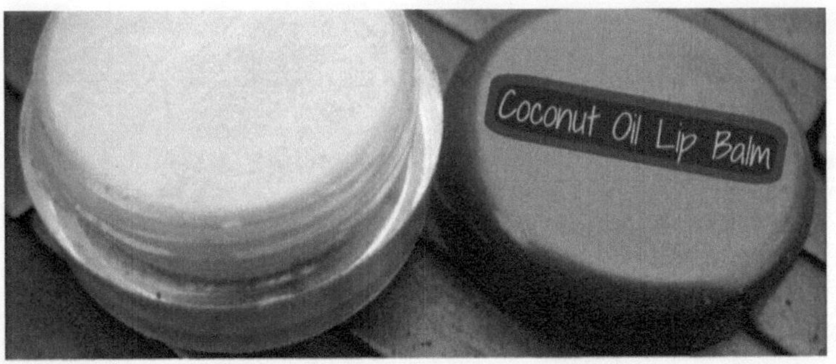

Materials

- 3 tablespoon olive oil

- 2 tablespoon coconut oil

- 1 tablespoon beeswax

- 1½ tablespoon cocoa butter

- 15 drops of peppermint oil

- ½ teaspoon of vitamin E

Directions

1. Ready your containers. Melt the coconut oil in a double boiler.

2. Stir in the almond oil and mix briskly.

3. Stir in the bees wax and cocoa butter until mixture is fully melted and mixed.

4. Add peppermint oil and vitamin E stir well.

5. Pour mixture into prepared containers.

33. Lemon Almond Lip Balm

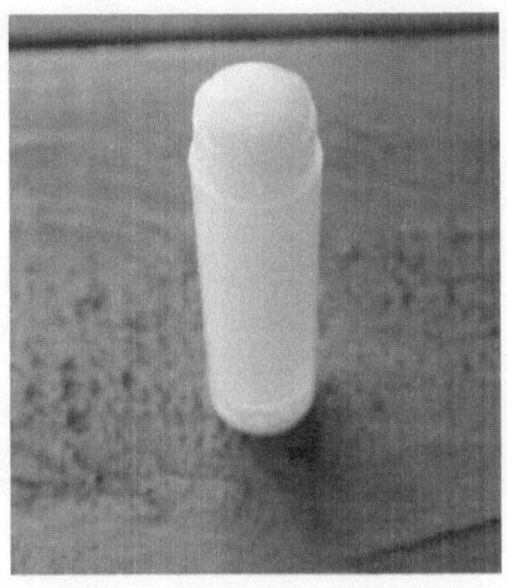

Materials

- 1 ½ tablespoon almond oil

- 1 ½ tablespoon coconut oil

- 1 ½ tablespoon grated beeswax

- 5 drops vitamin E

- 5 drops lime

- 5 drops lemon oil

Directions

1. Ready your lip balm containers. Melt beeswax and coconut oil in a double boiler or over a pot of boiling water.

2. Stir in the almond oil, and put the drops of lemon
   and lime oils and vitamin E and mix thoroughly.

3. Remove from heat and keep mixing for a short
   while.

4. Pour into pre-made containers.

5. Leave to cool overnight.

34. Honey & Sweet Orange Lip Balm

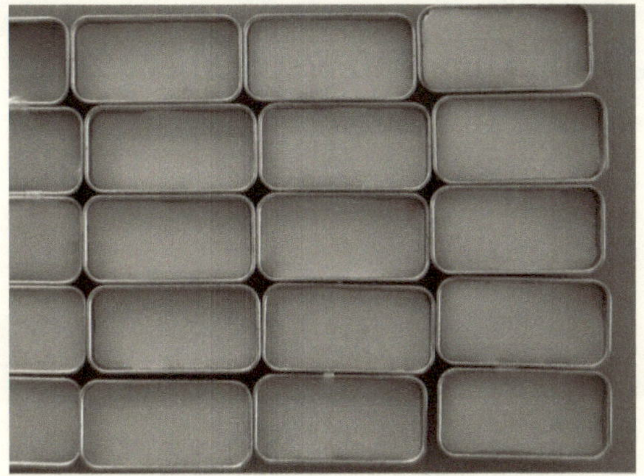

Materials

- 2 teaspoons petroleum jelly

- 5 drops of sweet orange oil

- 1 teaspoon honey

- 5 drops vitamin E

Directions

1. Prepare the lip balm containers.

2. Melt the petroleum jelly in a microwave friendly bowl for 30 seconds on medium heat.

3. Put the drops of vitamin E and those Lif sweet orange oil and mix thoroughly.

4. Add the honey and continue mixing so that honey
   does not set.

5. Pour the mixture into prepared containers and allow
   it to set.

35. Sunflower Rose Lip Balm

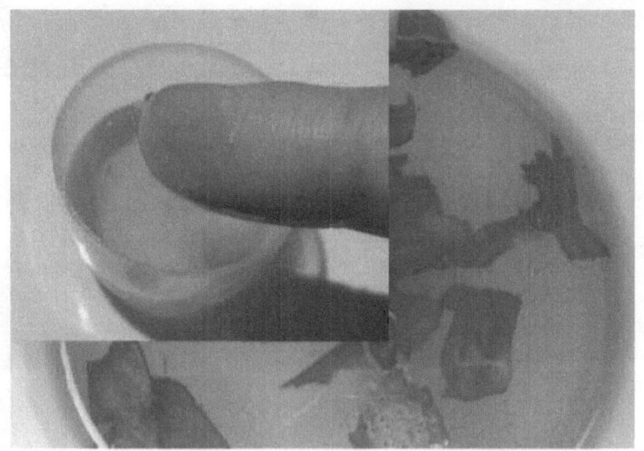

Materials

- 3 tablespoon sunflower oil

- 2 tablespoons shea butter

- 1½ tablespoon beeswax

- 1 tablespoon cocoa butter

- 10 -15 drops of rose oil

Directions

1. Prepare the containers. Melt the shea butter in a double boiler.

2. Add the sunflower oil and mix thoroughly.

3. Whisk in the bees wax and cocoa butter and transfer to very low heat stovetop.

4. Heat while stirring until mixture is fully melted and mixed.

5. Remove from heat and add rose oil, stir well. Pour into the readied containers.

Last Chance to Get YOUR Bonus!

FOR A LIMITED TIME ONLY – Get my best-selling book "DIY Crafts: The 100 Most Popular Crafts & Projects That Make Your Life Easier" absolutely FREE!

Readers who have downloaded the bonus book as well have seen the greatest changes in their crafting abilities and have expanded their repertoire of crafts – so it is *highly recommended* to get this bonus book today!

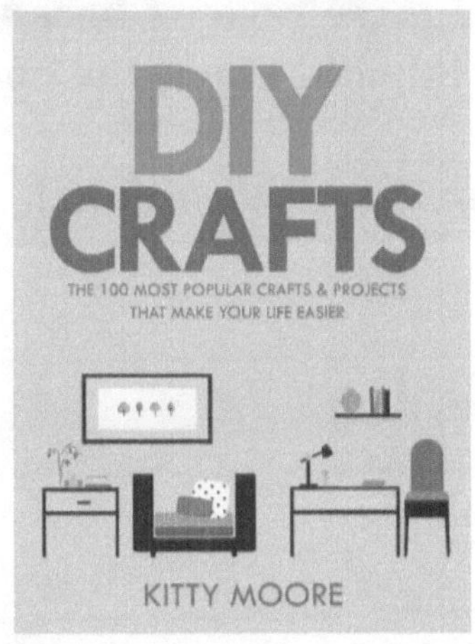

Get your free copy at:

ArtsCraftsAndMore.com/Bonus

Final Words

Thank you for downloading this book!

I really hope that you have been inspired to create your own projects and that you will have a lot of fun crafting.

I do hope that you and your family have found lots of ways to fill lazy afternoons or rainy days in a more fun way.

If you have enjoyed this book and would like to share your positive thoughts, could you please take 30 seconds of your time to go back and give me a review on my Amazon book page!

I really appreciate these reviews because I like to know what people have thought about the book.

Again, thank you and have fun crafting!

Disclaimer

No Warranties: The authors and publishers don't guarantee or warrant the quality, accuracy, completeness, timeliness, appropriateness or suitability of the information in this book, or of any product or services referenced by this site.

The information in this site is provided on an "as is" basis and the authors and publishers make no representations or warranties of any kind with respect to this information. This site may contain inaccuracies, typographical errors, or other errors.

Liability Disclaimer: The publishers, authors, and other parties involved in the creation, production, provision of information, or delivery of this site specifically disclaim any responsibility, and shall not be held liable for any damages, claims, injuries, losses, liabilities, costs, or obligations including any direct, indirect, special, incidental, or consequences damages (collectively known as "Damages") whatsoever and howsoever caused, arising out of, or in connection with the use or misuse of the site and the information contained within it, whether such Damages arise in contract, tort, negligence, equity, statute law, or by way of other legal theory.